Bridesmaid's Record Book

Written by Janet Brown
Illustrated by Lynne Willey

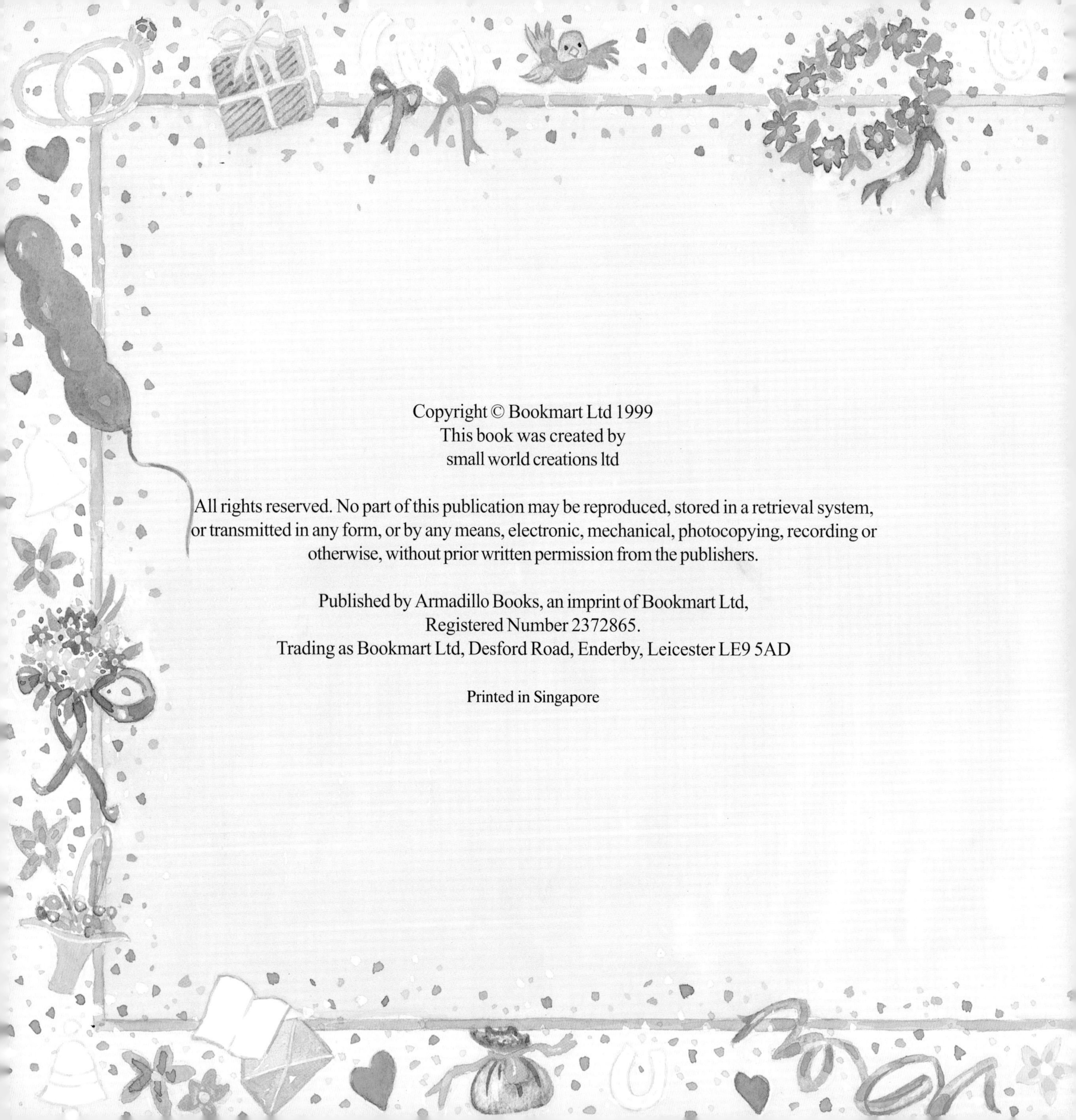

This book was created by
small world creations ltd

Published by Armadillo Books, an imprint of Bookmart Ltd,
Registered Number 2372865.
Trading as Bookmart Ltd, Desford Road, Enderby, Leicester LE9 5AD

Printed in Singapore

Contents

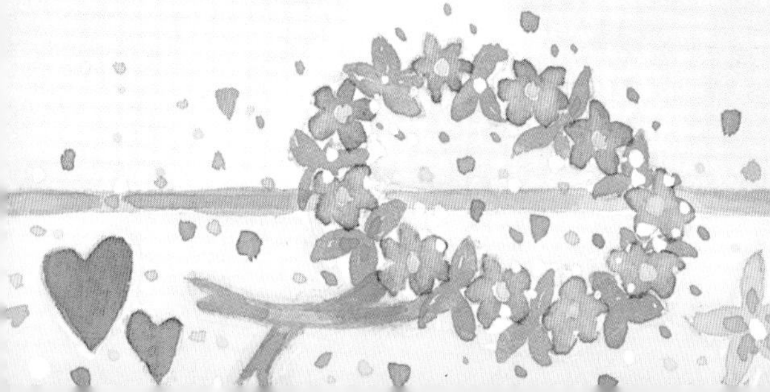

Introduction

For many young girls, being a bridesmaid is the most exciting thing they have done so far with their lives. This book will help to guide them – and their mothers! – through the events that will take place on the days leading up to the big day, and on the day itself.

Along the way they are encouraged to record each detail, through words, pictures and photographs.

Older bridesmaids will be able to fill in the details for themselves. Younger bridesmaids will require the help of their parents, but they should be encouraged to illustrate the words with photographs and their own drawings.

In the years to come, this book will serve as a wonderful souvenir of a very special day.

Your Details

*My name is:*____

You're going to be a bridesmaid!

Bridesmaids come in all shapes, sizes and ages.
You may be five or fifteen.
You may be asked to wear a traditional dress with a big bow and a head-dress, or a more casual outfit.
You may be the sole bridesmaid or one of several.

Whatever the details, whenever anyone looks at the wedding photographs in the years to come, there you will be, standing beside the bride!

On the day I am a bridesmaid

When you look back on yourself, will you remember what you were like on the day you were a bridesmaid?

Fill in the details here to make sure you don't forget.

This is how old I am:

This is how old my brothers and sisters are:

This is where I live:

This is my best friend:

This is the person I would most like to marry at this moment (you don't have to fill this part in if it's a secret):

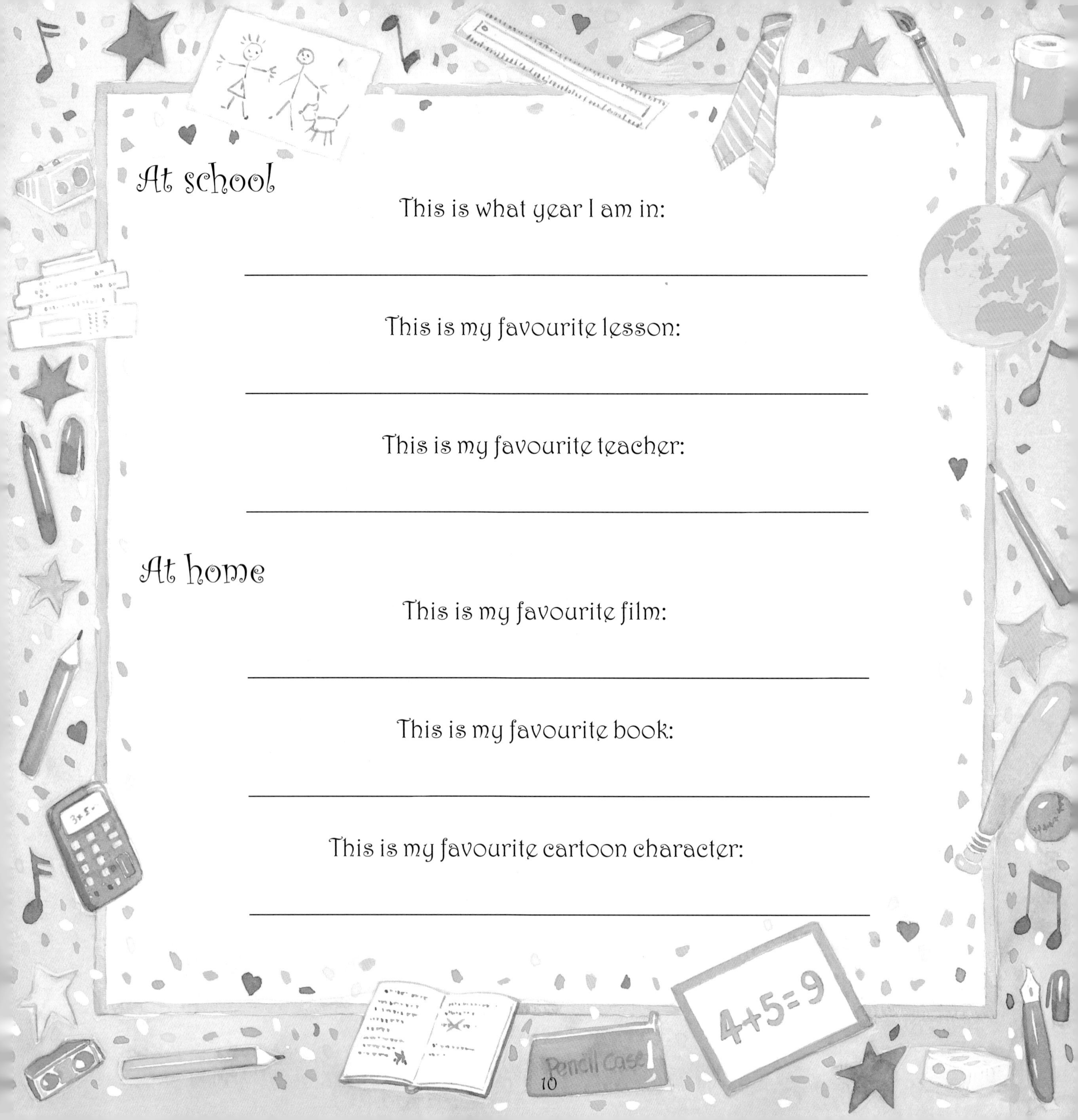

At school

This is what year I am in:

____

This is my favourite lesson:

____

This is my favourite teacher:

____

At home

This is my favourite film:

____

This is my favourite book:

____

This is my favourite cartoon character:

____

Here is a picture of me:

The Romance

Everyone loves a little romance!

Given your relationship with the bride, chances are that you have known for some time that a wedding was in the air.

Perhaps you were present when the bride and groom first met.

Perhaps they met at your party!

If you are the sister of the groom, maybe you knew that the bride was the girl for him before he did.

If you are closer to the bride, then you probably knew about the romance from day one.

Describe how you first met the bride/groom:

When did you first hear about the wedding:

Why You Were Asked

That's easy - because you are the person that the bride most wants to have standing near her on one of the most important days of her life!

You might be her sister or her niece, or her future sister-in-law or niece.

Perhaps you are close friends.

Or maybe you are new friends who are certain that you are going to know each other for a long time.

Whatever the relationship,
it's you that the bride will be counting on
to keep her calm, hold her flowers,
and help her look the best on her big day.

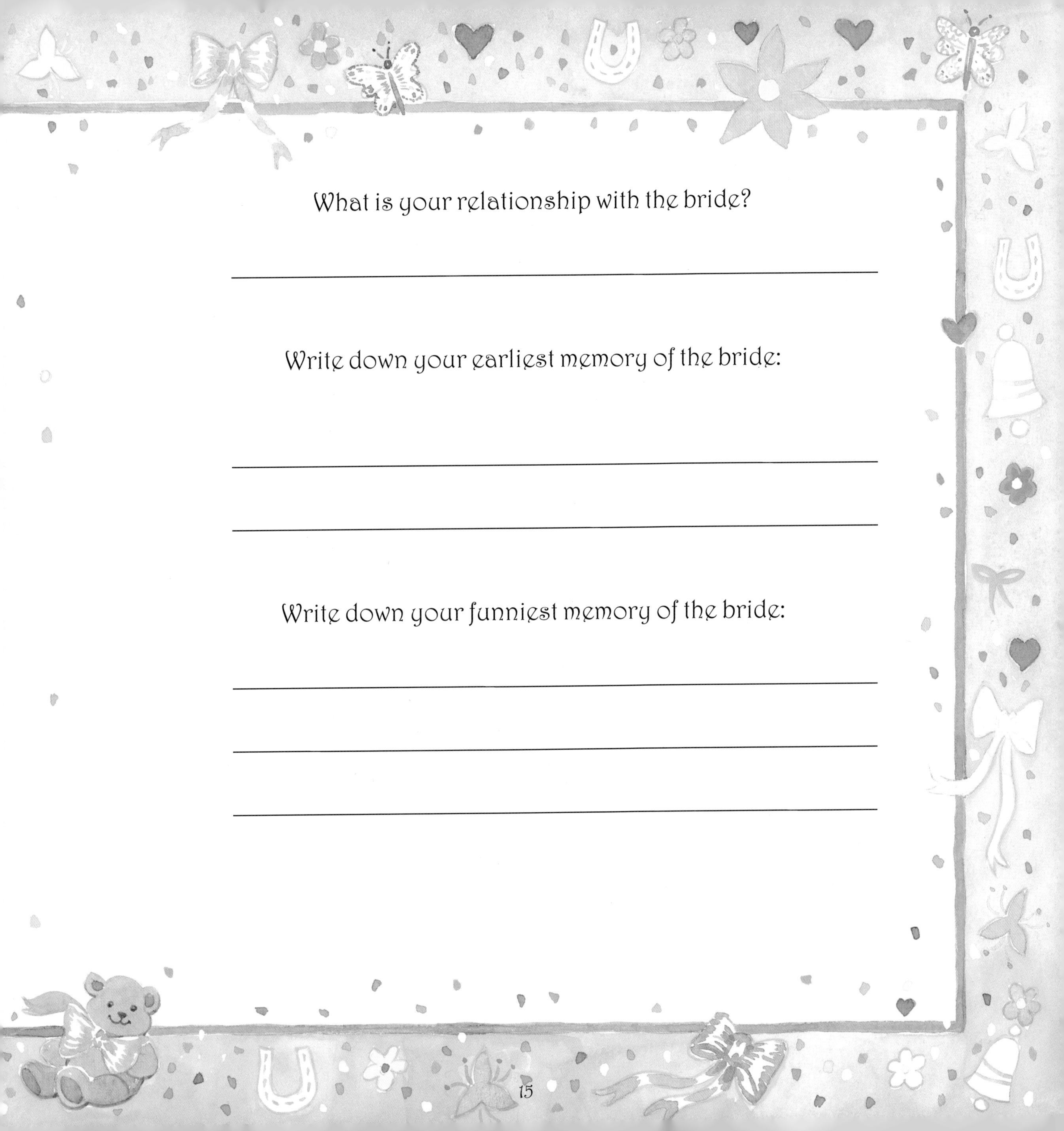

What is your relationship with the bride?

Write down your earliest memory of the bride:

Write down your funniest memory of the bride:

How You Were Asked

Some brides write their prospective bridesmaids a letter.

Others ask them on the telephone, or face-to-face.

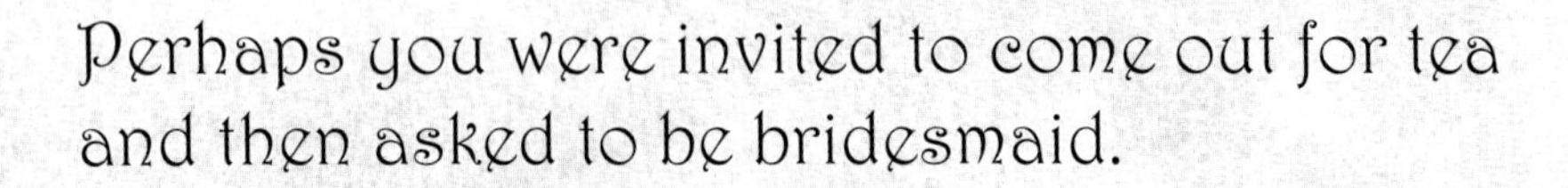

Perhaps you were invited to come out for tea
and then asked to be bridesmaid.

Maybe you were never asked at all -
maybe you were the natural choice
and it was taken for granted!

Who asked you to be the bridesmaid -
the bride, the groom or someone else?

How did they ask you - by letter, telephone or face-to-face?

Describe the scene:

Write down your exact reply:

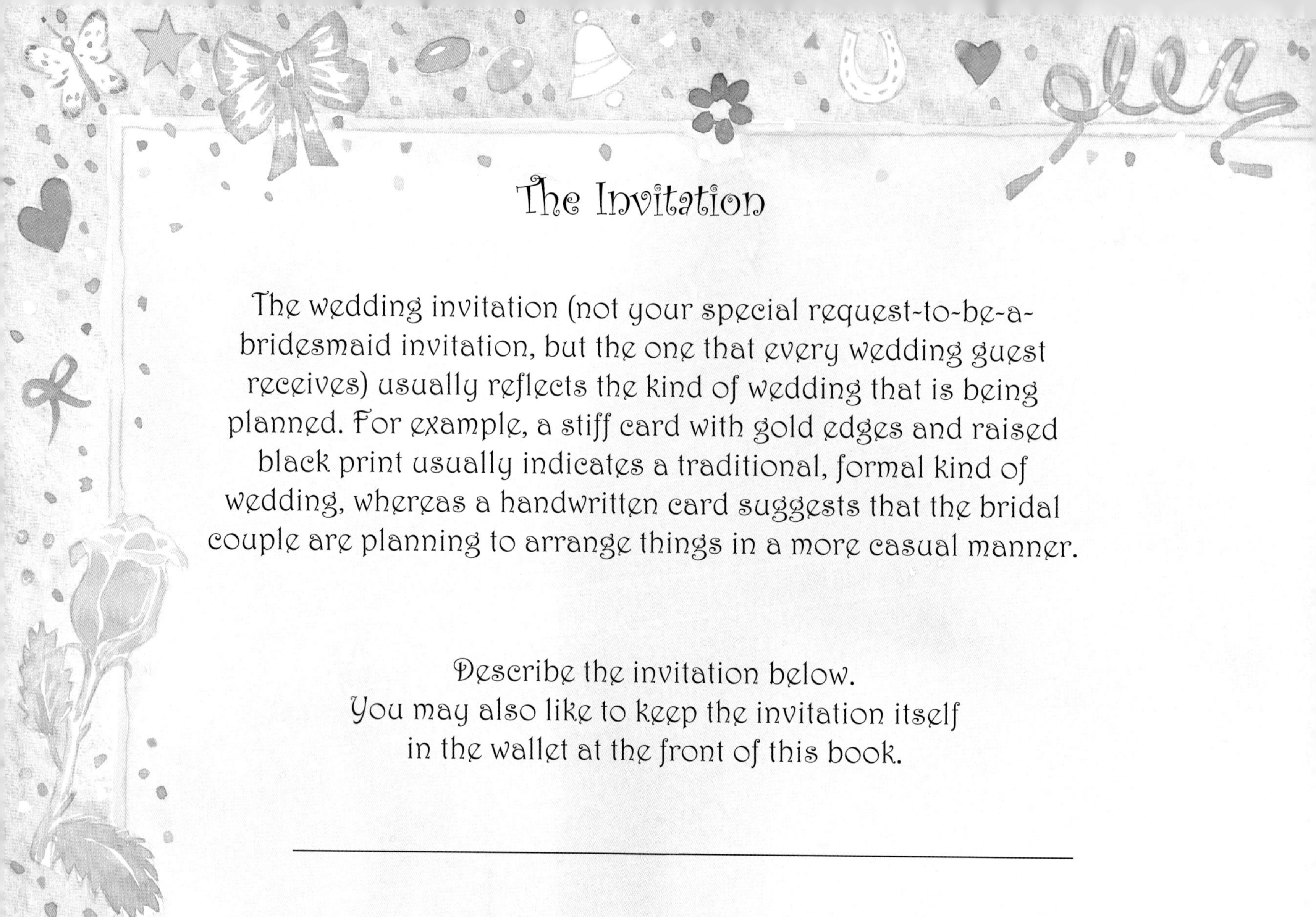

The Invitation

The wedding invitation (not your special request-to-be-a-bridesmaid invitation, but the one that every wedding guest receives) usually reflects the kind of wedding that is being planned. For example, a stiff card with gold edges and raised black print usually indicates a traditional, formal kind of wedding, whereas a handwritten card suggests that the bridal couple are planning to arrange things in a more casual manner.

Describe the invitation below.
You may also like to keep the invitation itself
in the wallet at the front of this book.

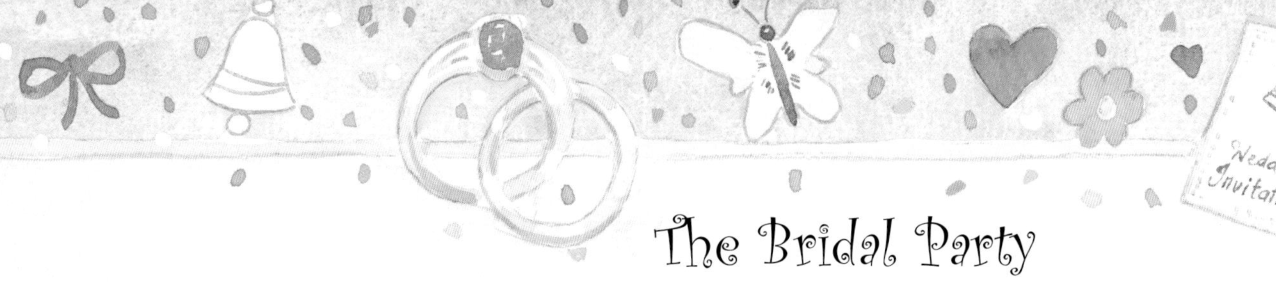

The Bridal Party

As bridesmaid, you will be an important part of the bridal party.
Other members of the party include the bride and groom, their parents,
the best man, and any other bridesmaids.

Write down the names of all the members of the bridal party:

The bride: ______________________

The groom: ______________________

The bride's parents:
____
____

The groom's parents:
____
____

The bridesmaids:
____
____

The best man:
____

Bridesmaid Duties

As a bridesmaid there are several duties that you will be expected to perform. In addition, the bride may have some special favours to ask you. If you are in any doubt about what is expected of you, write the bride a letter asking her exactly what role she wants you to play.

This is the kind of letter you might want to write:

Dear___________________ ,

I am really looking forward to being your bridesmaid on ________. I have been wondering about the role that you want me to play on the day. Can you let me know if there is anything special you would like me to do? For example, do you have a train that you need me to carry? Please let me know.

With love from________________

Special requests

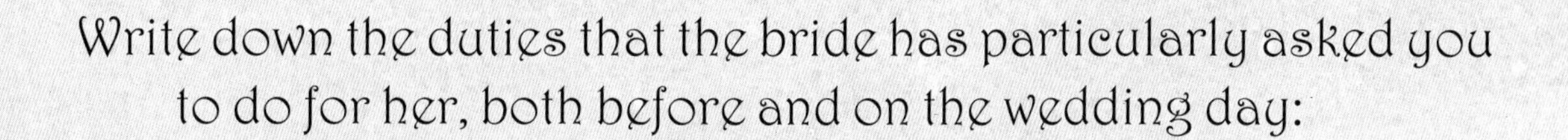

Write down the duties that the bride has particularly asked you to do for her, both before and on the wedding day:

Here are some of the more usual bridesmaid duties:

Before the ceremony

The bride will be nervous and forgetful on her wedding day. It may be your job to help her get dressed. For example, there may be a lot of buttons down the back of her dress. She may need someone to fetch and carry for her while she is getting dressed, and find all those little things that can get lost, like earrings.

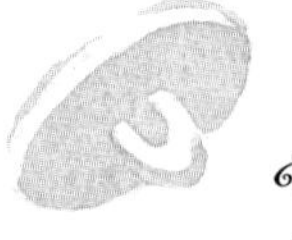

During the ceremony

If the bride's dress has long skirts or a train, you will need to make sure that they are straight and don't get caught on anything or trip her up as she walks. You may have to carry the train if it is very long.

During the ceremony you will usually be asked to hold the bride's flowers while she makes her vows and swaps rings with the groom.

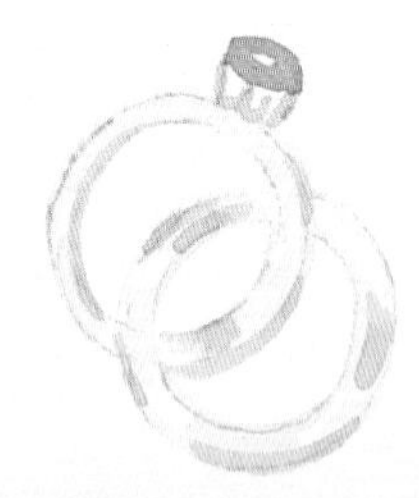

After the ceremony the photographs are taken.
You will be in lots of the photographs, so you need to make sure you are looking your best. You also need to keep an eye on the bride and make sure that her hair stays fixed, that the dress is straight and that she is holding her flowers.

(Brides often hold their flowers too high, which can hide the neckline of the dress. If the bride is doing this, you should advise her to lower the flowers to waist-height.)

At the reception

You may be required to take your place in the official line-up to greet the guests. There are several suggestions about what to say to each guest later in this book.

Remember that you are still on call during the reception, to look after flowers and run any little errands.
Your main job is still to make sure that the bride stays looking her best.

The Wedding Dress

The bride's choice of wedding dress dictates what everyone else will be wearing at the wedding. If she is wearing a traditional, long, white dress with a veil, chances are that you will be wearing a long dress too. If the bride is more casually dressed in a short dress or a suit, you will be wearing something to complement her outfit.

Usually the bride will tell you what she wants you to wear. But try to find out as early as possible what kind of dress she is planning.

A wedding dress can be floaty and romantic...

...or straight and elegant.

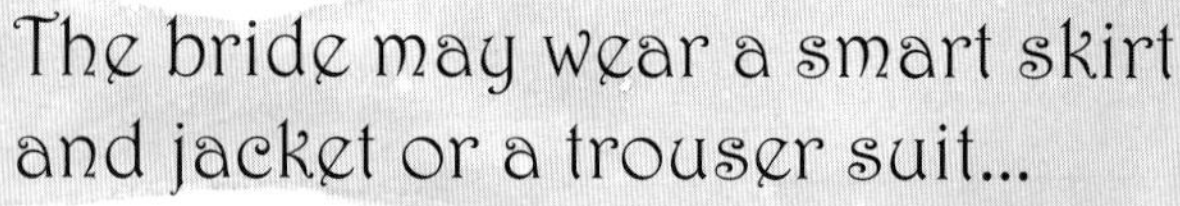

The bride may wear a smart skirt
and jacket or a trouser suit...

...or she may decide to be
completely unconventional!

As soon as you know the details of the bride's wedding dress, write them down here and then draw a picture:

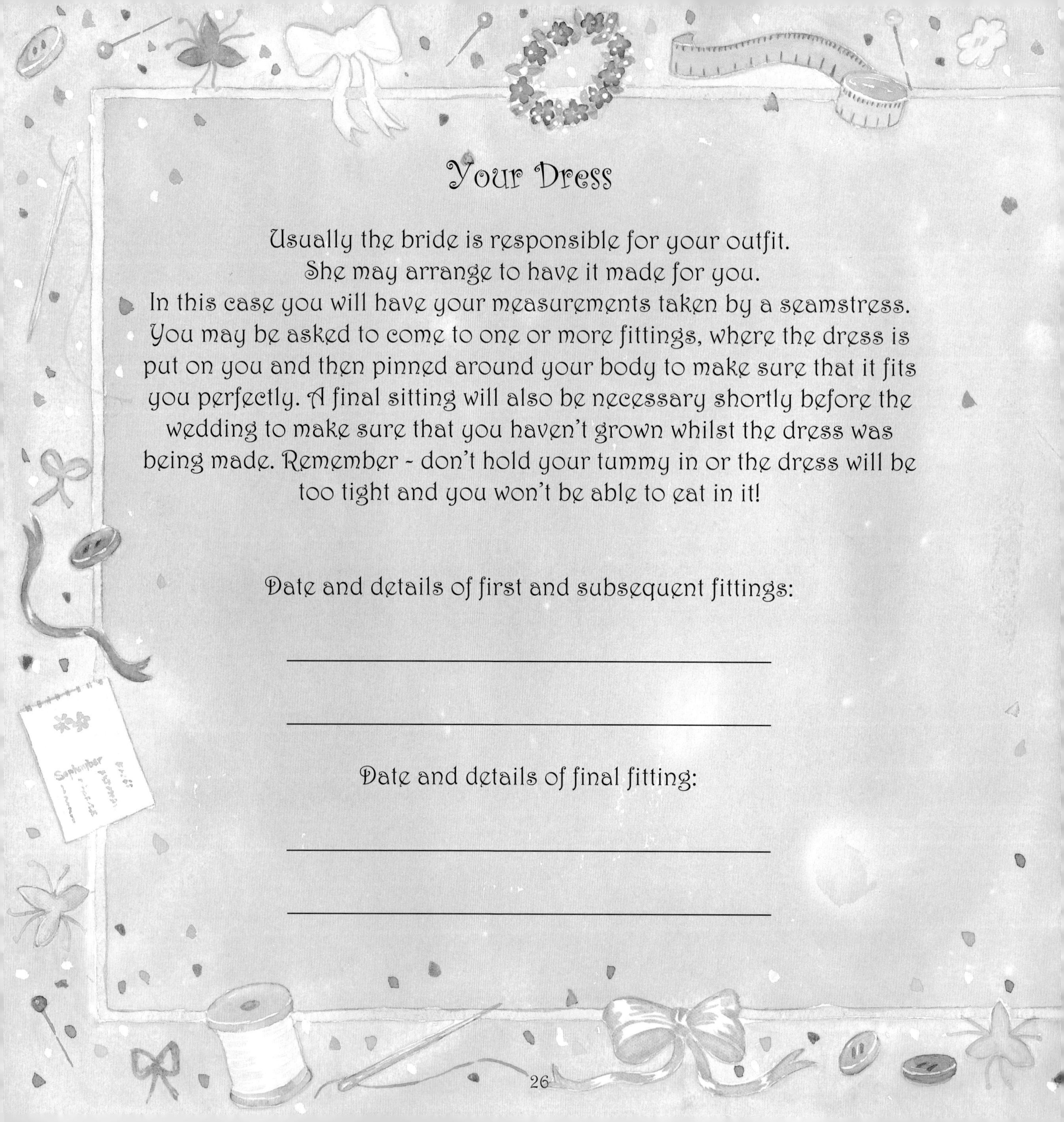

Your Dress

Usually the bride is responsible for your outfit.
She may arrange to have it made for you.
In this case you will have your measurements taken by a seamstress.
You may be asked to come to one or more fittings, where the dress is put on you and then pinned around your body to make sure that it fits you perfectly. A final sitting will also be necessary shortly before the wedding to make sure that you haven't grown whilst the dress was being made. Remember - don't hold your tummy in or the dress will be too tight and you won't be able to eat in it!

Date and details of first and subsequent fittings:

____

____

Date and details of final fitting:

____

____

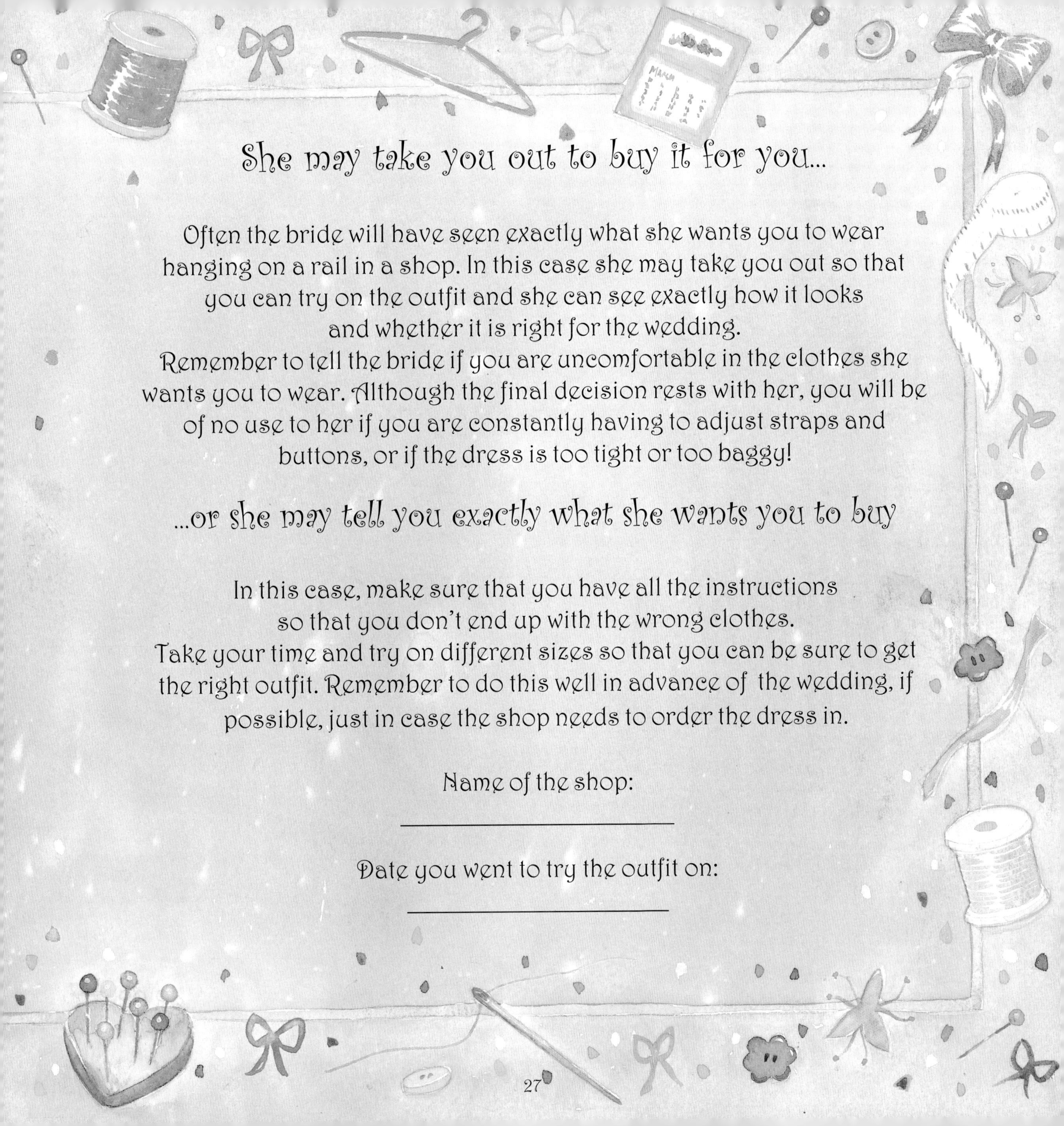

She may take you out to buy it for you...

Often the bride will have seen exactly what she wants you to wear hanging on a rail in a shop. In this case she may take you out so that you can try on the outfit and she can see exactly how it looks and whether it is right for the wedding.

Remember to tell the bride if you are uncomfortable in the clothes she wants you to wear. Although the final decision rests with her, you will be of no use to her if you are constantly having to adjust straps and buttons, or if the dress is too tight or too baggy!

...or she may tell you exactly what she wants you to buy

In this case, make sure that you have all the instructions so that you don't end up with the wrong clothes.

Take your time and try on different sizes so that you can be sure to get the right outfit. Remember to do this well in advance of the wedding, if possible, just in case the shop needs to order the dress in.

Name of the shop:

____

Date you went to try the outfit on:

____

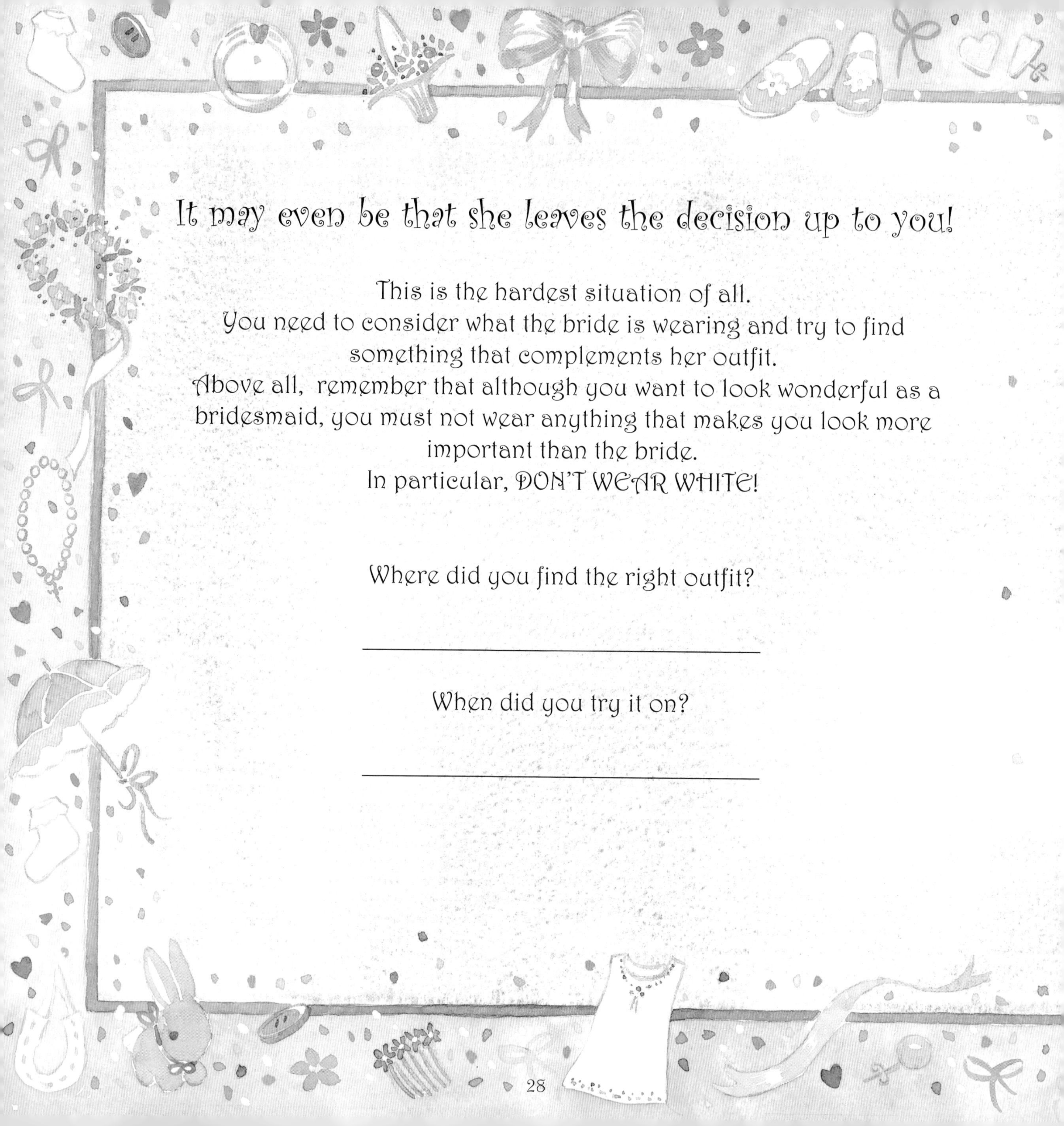

It may even be that she leaves the decision up to you!

This is the hardest situation of all.
You need to consider what the bride is wearing and try to find something that complements her outfit.
Above all, remember that although you want to look wonderful as a bridesmaid, you must not wear anything that makes you look more important than the bride.
In particular, DON'T WEAR WHITE!

Where did you find the right outfit?

____

When did you try it on?

____

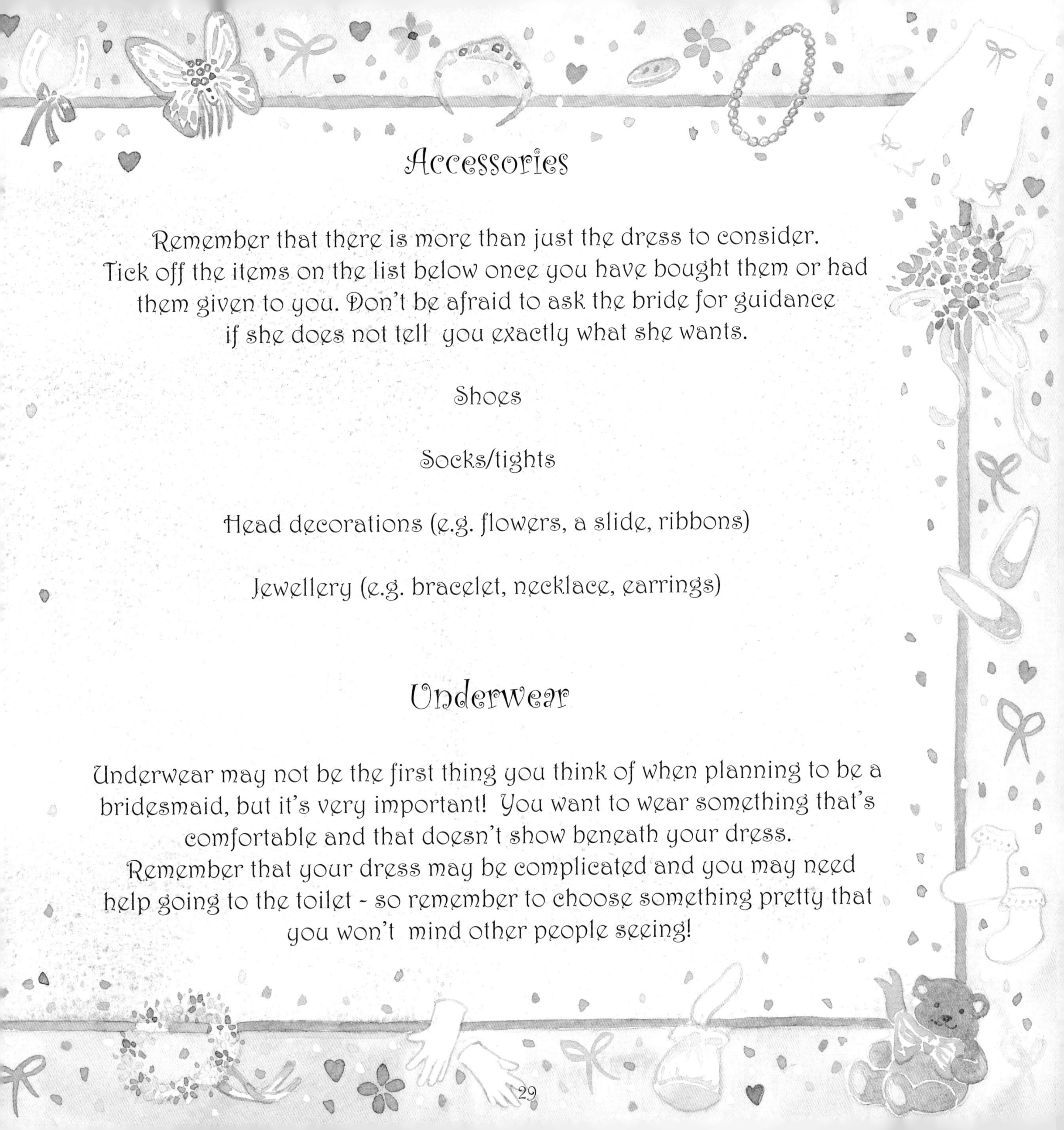

Accessories

Remember that there is more than just the dress to consider. Tick off the items on the list below once you have bought them or had them given to you. Don't be afraid to ask the bride for guidance if she does not tell you exactly what she wants.

Shoes

Socks/tights

Head decorations (e.g. flowers, a slide, ribbons)

Jewellery (e.g. bracelet, necklace, earrings)

Underwear

Underwear may not be the first thing you think of when planning to be a bridesmaid, but it's very important! You want to wear something that's comfortable and that doesn't show beneath your dress. Remember that your dress may be complicated and you may need help going to the toilet - so remember to choose something pretty that you won't mind other people seeing!

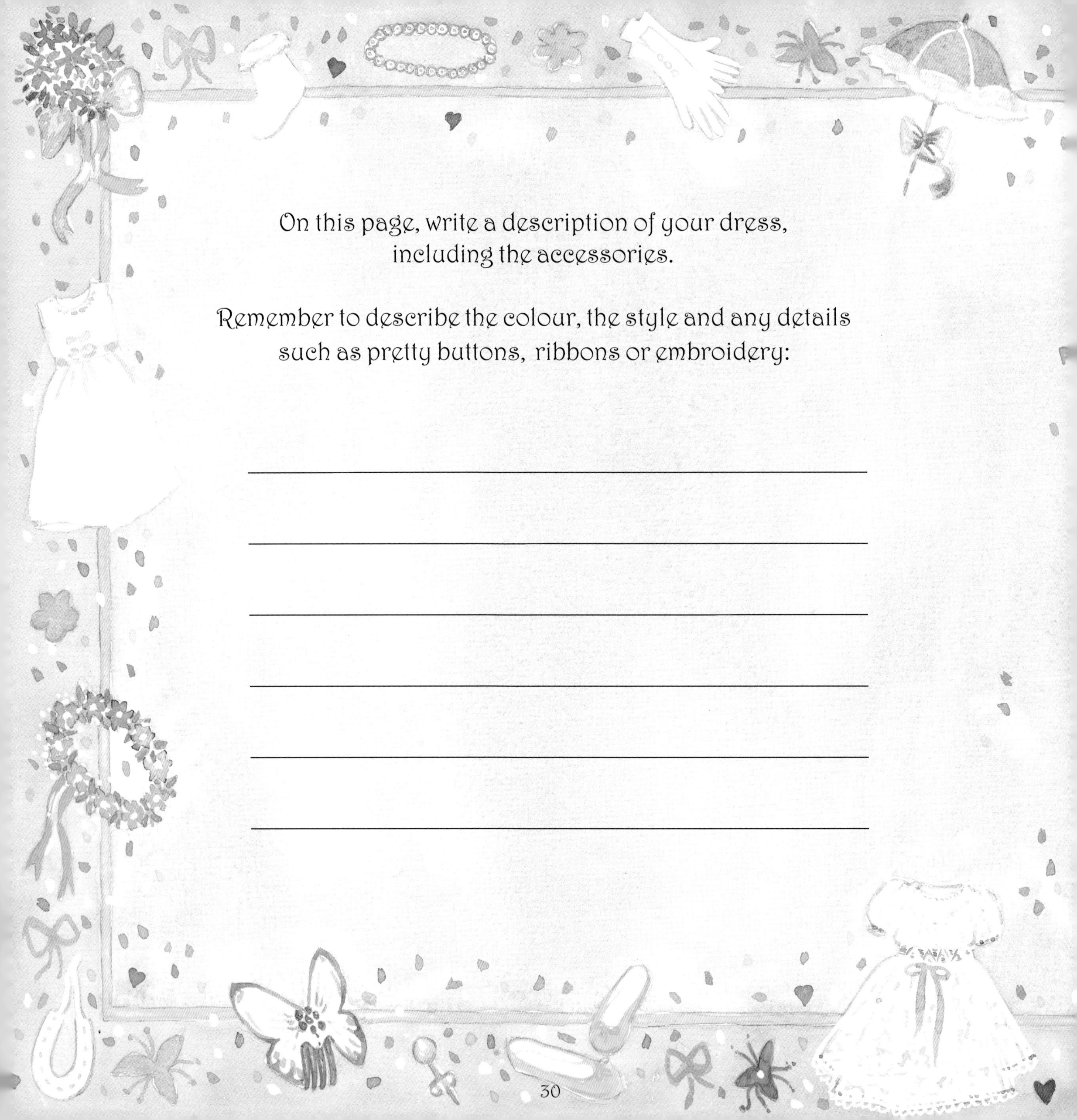

On this page, write a description of your dress, including the accessories.

Remember to describe the colour, the style and any details such as pretty buttons, ribbons or embroidery:

____

____

____

____

____

____

On this page draw a picture
or paste a photograph of your dress.

The Ceremony

There are lots of different wedding ceremonies available and it's up to the bride and groom to decide how they want to go about it.

They may choose to get married in a church...

... or at a Registry Office.

They may decide to get married in a marquee ...

... or outside under the blue sky!

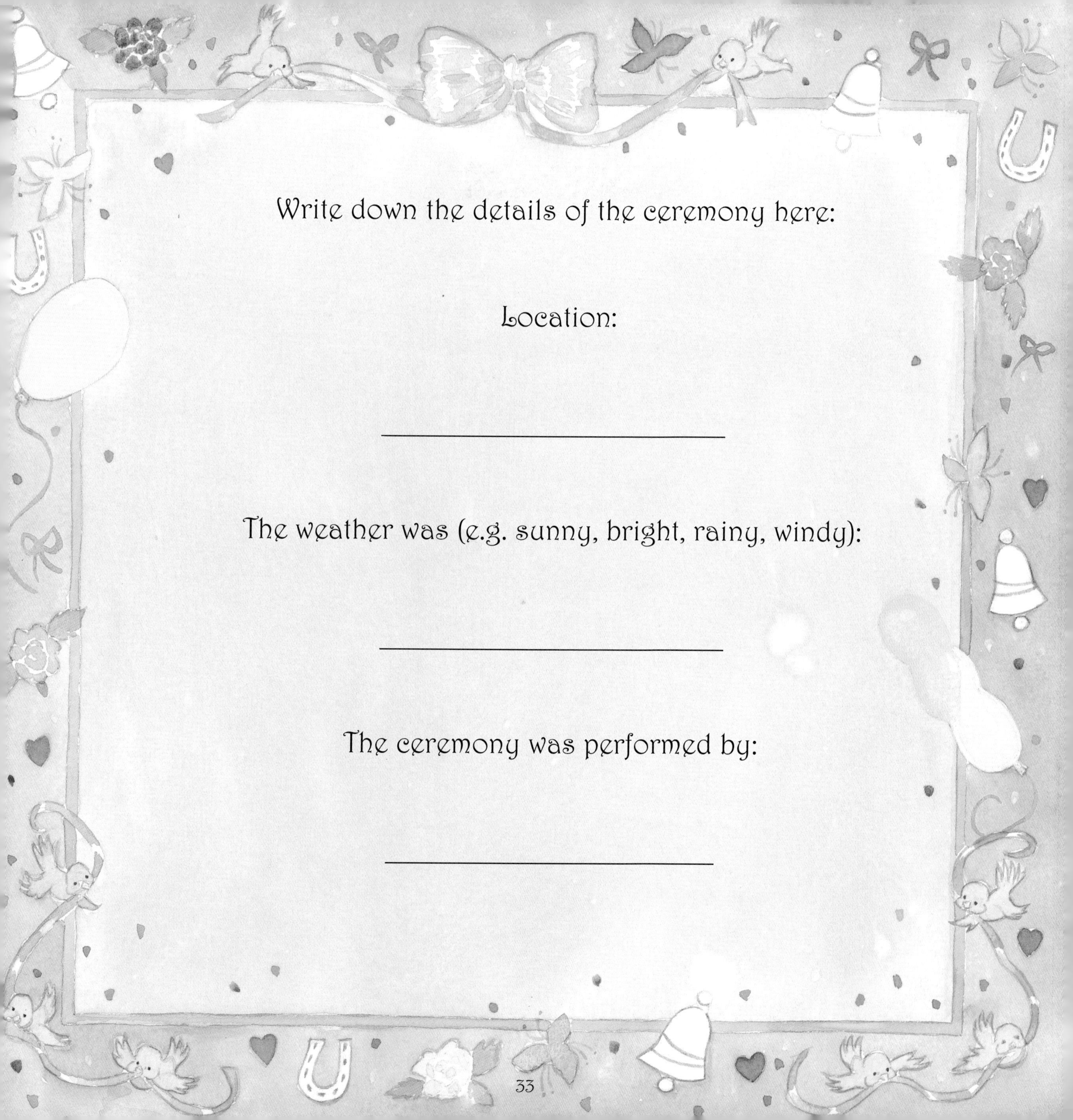

Write down the details of the ceremony here:

Location:

____

The weather was (e.g. sunny, bright, rainy, windy):

____

The ceremony was performed by:

____

The Order of Service

It is usual at weddings for each guest to be given a leaflet containing details of the ceremony - for example, an order of service, the words of the hymns or songs that are going to be sung, or a special prayer or poem for the bridal couple.

You may like to keep the Order of Service in the wallet at the front of this book.

Music

At some ceremonies there may be live music - for example, an organ or trumpets or a piano or guitars. Often everyone will be involved in singing a song or a hymn.

What kind of music was played?

____

What songs did you sing?

____

Readings

At some ceremonies, invited guests may come up to the front to perform a reading - for example a religious piece or a poem or a piece of prose.

Who performed the readings?

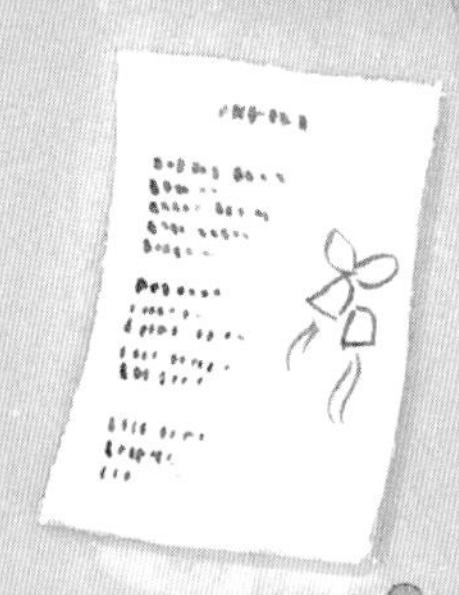

What did they read?

Photographs

Although having your picture taken can be lots of fun, this part of the wedding can take a long time. Since you will be in many of the pictures, you need to be patient and ready to smile until your face aches! Remember that these pictures are for the bride and groom to keep forever.

How many pictures were you in?

The Reception

The ceremony is over and it's time for the new husband and wife to celebrate with their friends and family!

Welcome Line

At some weddings the bride and groom and those nearest to them form a line and greet each guest in turn as they arrive for the reception. As bridesmaid, you will probably be part of this line-up. This means that you have to shake everybody's hand and swap a few words with them. Try not to talk to anybody for too long as this holds up the line. Here's the kind of thing you might want to say:

"Wasn't it a nice ceremony?"
"Doesn't the bride look beautiful?"
"It's lovely to see you!"
"Welcome to the reception."

Dining

If there is a sit-down meal, you may be seated at the head table with the bridal party. Alternatively, there might be a buffet, or drinks and canapes. Whatever the arrangement, try to mingle with as many people as possible and be polite and friendly - you are still the bride's right hand woman! In particular, make sure you talk to the best man at some stage, since he is your "opposite number" in the bridal party.

Who did you sit with during the meal?

____

What did you have to eat?

____

Speeches

Usually the following people make formal speeches at the reception: the best man, the bride's father and the groom.

Often, the floor is then thrown open to anyone else who has something special to say to the bride and groom.

During the speeches, it is normal for the groom to make a toast to the bridesmaid - for helping to make the day special. Make sure you haven't disappeared off somewhere during the groom's speech!

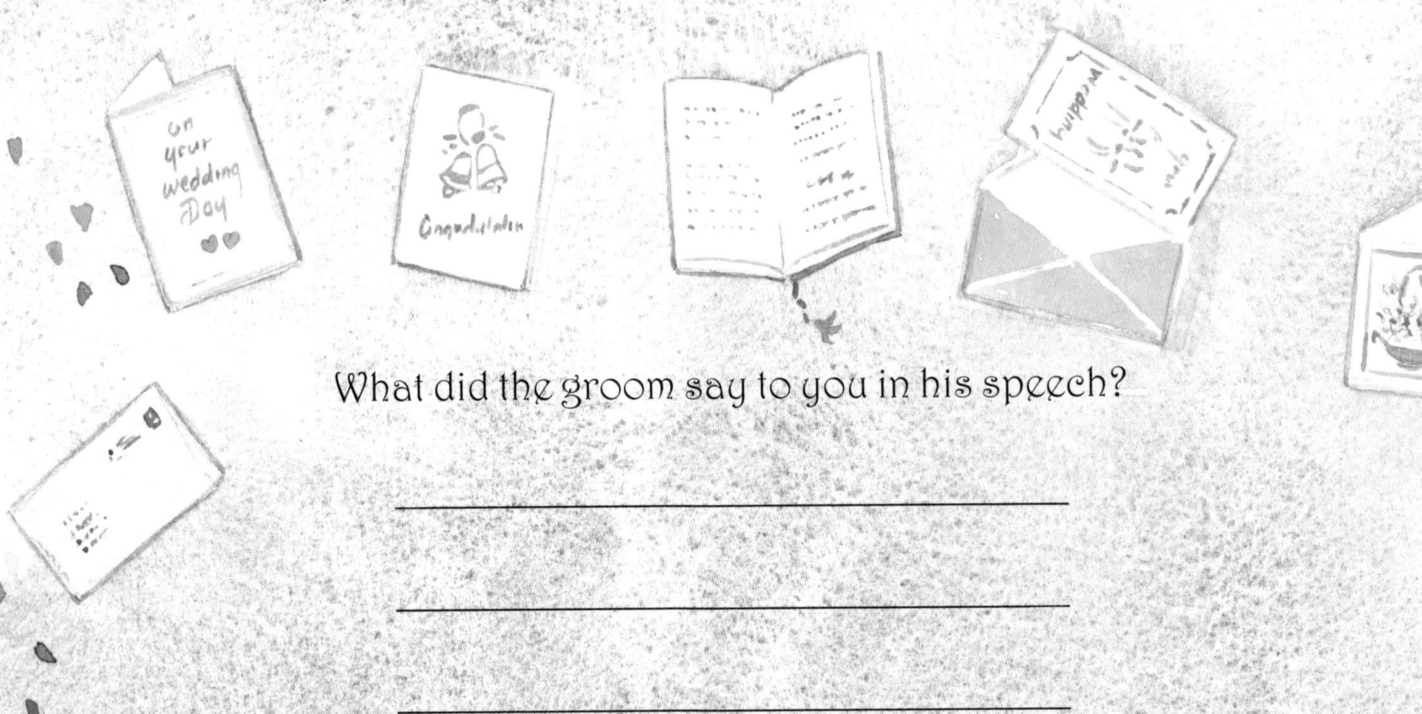

What did the groom say to you in his speech?

____

____

____

The Entertainment

It is common to have some kind of a party after the reception,
either immediately following a meal
or perhaps as a separate event in the evening.

What kind of entertainment was there after the reception (e.g. disco)?

____

If there was dancing, who did you dance with?

____

If there was live music, what was the name of the group/singer?

____

The Guests

Weddings are a great time for family and friends to get together. If you know the bride well, or if you are related to her, chances are you will know lots of people at the wedding. However, this is also a chance to talk to new people and make new friends.

Write down here the names of everyone you can remember that was at the wedding. Put a tick beside those you already knew, and a star beside those you met for the first time.

____

____

____

____

____

Choosing a Gift

Being a bridesmaid at a wedding is one of the biggest and best presents you can give to a bride and groom. However, you may wish to give them something to keep as well.

The Wedding List

Many couples have a wedding list. This is a list of items which they would like to receive from their wedding guests. These items may all be available from one shop, or from several shops.

Usually someone will arrange this for you, but you should know the details in case they need advice:

- Find out which shop holds the couple's wedding list. (Often this information will be sent out with the invitation.)

- Ring up the shop and tell the shop how much you want to spend. They will tell you what's on the list within that price range.

- Choose your gift and pay for it, either on the phone or by sending your money.

Choosing your own gift

For a more personal touch, you may want to find something yourself.
You may choose an ornament you know they particularly like.
Remember that the gift is for the bride and groom, so something for their home is usually a good idea.
Here are some suggestions to get you started:

. romantic candles
. photograph frames
. an embroidered tablecloth
. a picture
. pretty cushion covers
. a piece of porcelain

Making a gift

Alternatively, you may want to make them something. For example:

. You could draw or paint a picture and have it nicely framed.
. You could make them a papier mâché figure, and paint it.
. You could make some pretty vases by painting empty jam-jars or glass containers.
. You could write them a little poem, and decorate the edges of the page with pretty illustrations.
(You might like to copy the decoration on these pages, for example.)

What gift did you give the bride and groom?

____

Thank-You Letters

It's all over and you've hung away the dress. But you've got this book, some lovely photographs, and your memories to remind you of the day you were bridesmaid.

But wait - there's one last task you have to do!
You might have to write your thank - you letter to the bride and groom.
Here are some things you might like to say:

Dear .... ,

Thank you for a lovely time on________. I had a wonderful day,
and thought everything went very well.
You were a beautiful bride and it was an honour to be your
bridesmaid. Thank you for everything.

Love ....

Dear .... ,

I will always remember your special day.
Thank you very much for inviting me to be your bridesmaid.
I thought you looked wonderful together
and I hope you will be very happy.

Love ....

Dear .... ,

Thank you for your special gift
and asking me to be your bridesmaid.
It was a wonderful day and I will always remember it.

Love ....

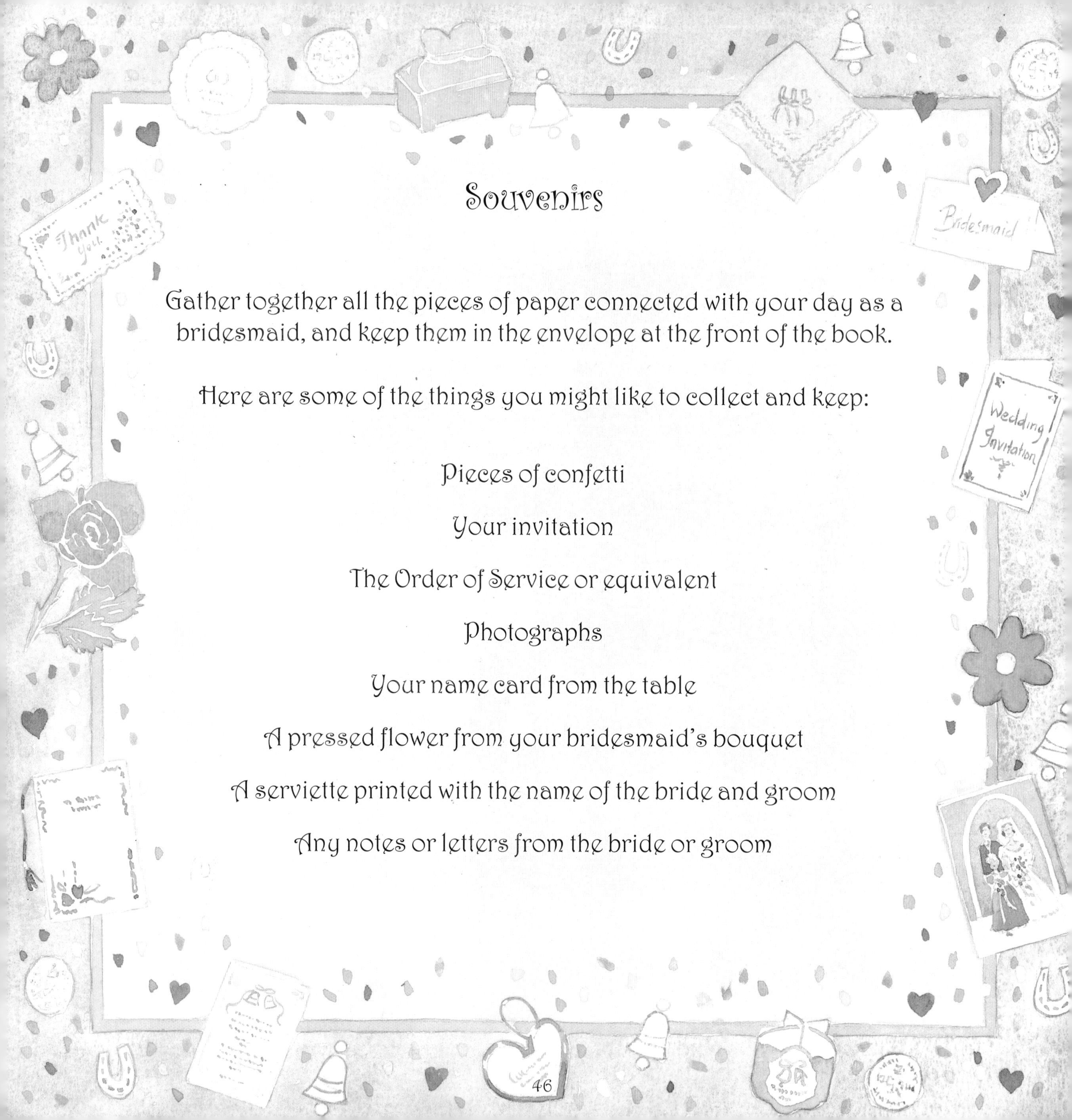

Souvenirs

Gather together all the pieces of paper connected with your day as a bridesmaid, and keep them in the envelope at the front of the book.

Here are some of the things you might like to collect and keep:

Pieces of confetti

Your invitation

The Order of Service or equivalent

Photographs

Your name card from the table

A pressed flower from your bridesmaid's bouquet

A serviette printed with the name of the bride and groom

Any notes or letters from the bride or groom